D1288475

Easy
505.775

514.775 PETRIE
5 - 13 - 11  Mid American Book  c.1  $17.95  14475 PETRIE

ABDO Publishing Company

# BUGS!
## Fleas

Kristin Petrie

LIBRARY

## visit us at
## www.abdopublishing.com

Published by ABDO Publishing Company, 8000 West 78th Street, Edina, Minnesota 55439.
Copyright © 2009 by Abdo Consulting Group, Inc. International copyrights reserved in all
countries. No part of this book may be reproduced in any form without written permission from the
publisher. The Checkerboard Library™ is a trademark and logo of ABDO Publishing Company.

Printed in the United States.

Cover Photo: Corbis
Interior Photos: Alamy pp. 7, 13, 19, 26, 28, 29; Animals Animals p. 15; Corbis pp. 1, 5, 9, 24-25;
    iStockphoto pp. 4, 21; National Geographic Image Collection pp. 19, 23; Photo Researchers
    pp. 10, 11, 17, 19, 21

Series Coordinator: BreAnn Rumsch
Editors: Megan M. Gunderson, BreAnn Rumsch
Art Direction & Cover Design: Neil Klinepier

### Library of Congress Cataloging-in-Publication Data

Petrie, Kristin, 1970-
  Fleas / Kristin Petrie.
      p. cm. -- (Bugs!)
  Includes index.
  ISBN 978-1-60453-067-4
  1. Fleas--Juvenile literature. I. Title.

  QL599.5.P48 2008
  595.77'5--dc22

                        2008004790

# Contents

# Frightful Fleas

*If your pet is constantly scratching, it might have fleas!*

When we think of fleas, most of us think of dogs and cats. Flea-ridden pets look miserable and scratch nonstop. Do you know why they are so unhappy?

It is because fleas are sucking their blood! Yes, Fido and Fluffy are food to bloodsucking fleas. Fleas are called **ectoparasites**. They live on the skin, fur, or feathers of an animal called a host. Fleas feed on the host's blood, skin cells, and feathers.

When fleas bite, they **inject** their **saliva** into a host. Yuck! That is what makes flea bites so itchy. Scratching the bites can cause an **infection**. In addition, some fleas can transmit serious diseases.

It is important to understand fleas. The more you learn, the easier it will be to prevent an **infestation**. You can protect your dog, your cat, and yourself from these troublesome bloodsuckers!

A flea uses its bloodsucking mouthparts to hang onto its host's skin.

# What Are They?

Fleas are insects.  Like all insects, they belong to the class Insecta.  Within this class, fleas belong to the order Siphonaptera.  This scientific name comes from words meaning "hollow tube" and "wingless."  The order Siphonaptera is divided into seven families.  The common flea and rodent flea families are two examples.

Each flea family includes many different flea species.  All together, there are about 2,000 flea species in the world.  More than 300 of these species exist in North America.

Each species of flea has a two-word name called a binomial.  A binomial combines the genus with a descriptive name, or epithet.  For example, a bat flea's binomial is *Ischnopsyllus octactenus*.

Some species, such as the rabbit flea, like to stick with just one type of host.  Other species are not as choosy.  For example, the cat flea can be found on cats, dogs, and people!  However, some animals are not tasty to fleas.  Apes, monkeys, and horses are among the animals whose blood fleas do not like.

The cat flea accounts for almost all fleas found on cats and dogs in the United States.

## THAT'S CLASSIFIED!

SCIENTISTS USE A METHOD CALLED SCIENTIFIC CLASSIFICATION TO SORT THE WORLD'S LIVING ORGANISMS INTO GROUPS. EIGHT GROUPS MAKE UP THE BASIC CLASSIFICATION SYSTEM. IN DESCENDING ORDER, THEY ARE DOMAIN, KINGDOM, PHYLUM, CLASS, ORDER, FAMILY, GENUS, AND SPECIES.

THE PHRASE "DEAR KING PHILIP, COME OUT FOR GOODNESS' SAKE!" MAY HELP YOU REMEMBER THIS ORDER. THE FIRST LETTER OF EACH WORD IS A CLUE FOR EACH GROUP.

DOMAIN IS THE MOST BASIC GROUP. SPECIES IS THE MOST SPECIFIC GROUP. MEMBERS OF A SPECIES SHARE COMMON CHARACTERISTICS. YET, THEY ARE DIFFERENT FROM ALL OTHER LIVING THINGS IN AT LEAST ONE WAY.

# Body Parts

Fleas are very small. They range from the size of a pinhead to that of a sunflower seed. Fleas have flattened sides, like the body of a fish. This narrow shape allows fleas to move easily through a host's hair or feathers.

A thick skin called an exoskeleton covers the flea's body. The exoskeleton is very hard. It protects the flea's insides and gives the flea its shape. It also makes the flea resistant to animal claws and human fingers.

The flea's body is divided into three body **segments**. These are the head, the thorax, and the abdomen. All three segments are covered in hairs and **spines**. The flea's sensory hairs pick up information from its **environment**.

Spines anchor the flea to its host. These spines point toward the flea's rear end. When a cat or a dog scratches, the spines catch on their fur. This helps the flea stay on your pet.

**BUG BYTES**

*Female fleas are always larger than the males of their species.*

A flea's sensory hairs can detect the breath and the body heat of a nearby host.

The head is the first and smallest body **segment**. It features eyes, antennae, and a mouth. Some fleas have simple, weak eyes called ocelli. They only sense light and dark. Many fleas do not have eyes at all.

Since fleas cannot see, they use their short, jointed antennae to get around. Antennae can smell things in the flea's surroundings. The flea uses its sense of smell to find food, shelter, and a mate.

For such a tiny insect, the flea has **complex** mouthparts. A set of large, feelerlike

*A female's sharp mouthparts allow her to consume much food. She may eat 15 times her body weight in blood every day.*

palpi are used to locate and taste a possible snack. When the flea is ready to eat, several parts work together.

Smaller palpi help support and guide the flea's long, piercing stylet. This stylet is made of two bladelike laciniae and a needlelike epipharynx. The blades cut the host's skin. Then, the epipharynx slips into the wound to obtain food.

Next, the **salivary** glands start working. The laciniae form a

small channel for the flea's saliva to flow into the wound. The flea's spit prevents the host's blood from clotting. Finally, the laciniae and the epipharynx combine to form a channel. Pumps inside the flea's body suck blood up through the channel.

The next body **segment** is the thorax. Usually, an insect's thorax features wings and legs. However, fleas break this rule. That is because they are wingless. A flea's legs are so powerful that they do not need wings to get around!

Like all insects, a flea has six legs. Each leg ends with a claw. The claws help the flea stay buried in its host's hair and other surfaces. These include bedding, clothing, carpet, and furniture.

The first pair of legs is the shortest. The second pair is slightly longer. These four legs are mainly used for grasping. The last set of legs is for jumping.

The long back legs have strong muscles. These muscles store large amounts of energy. When released, the enormous burst of energy sends the flea through the air like a rubber band!

Beyond the flea's thorax is its abdomen. The abdomen is made of several segments of exoskeleton. It is the largest of the three body segments. Many of the flea's **organs** are located there.

**BUG BYTES**

*The largest known flea is the North American* Hystrichopsylla schefferi. *It measures .47 inches (1.2 cm) long!*

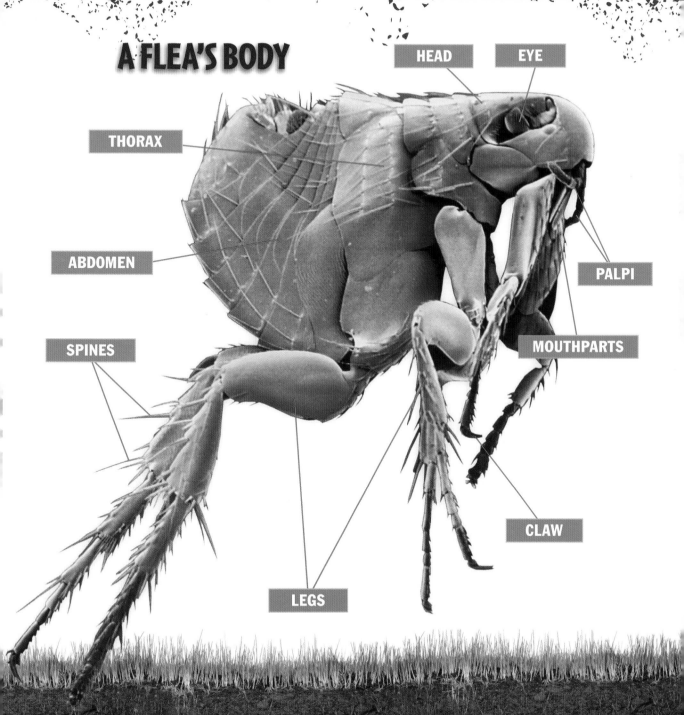

# A FLEA'S BODY

HEAD

EYE

THORAX

ABDOMEN

PALPI

SPINES

MOUTHPARTS

LEGS

CLAW

# The Inside Story

Inside a flea, several important systems work together to keep its tiny body moving. These systems help the flea breathe, move, and sense its **environment**.

Like other insects, fleas do not breathe with lungs. Instead, their respiratory system uses spiracles and tracheae. Oxygen enters a flea's body through holes along its sides called spiracles. Inside, tubes called tracheae connect to the spiracles. These tubes deliver air throughout the flea's body.

Fleas have an open circulatory system and a simple heart. This means that blood flows freely through a flea's body. Flea blood is called hemolymph. The heart pumps the hemolymph from one end of the flea's body to the other.

A simple nervous system controls a flea's movements and sense **organs**. The flea's brain connects to clusters of **nerves** called ganglia. The ganglia extend from the brain to nerves in the thorax and the abdomen.

A flea can jump forward more than 12 inches (30 cm). That is equal to 200 times its body length! It can also jump 8 inches (20 cm) straight up in the air.

# Transformation

Like many insects, fleas go through a four-stage life cycle. The stages are egg, larva, pupa, and adult. This process is called complete **metamorphosis**.

Insects with this type of life cycle make an amazing transformation. They begin as eggs, hatch into wormy creatures, and then go into hiding. There, many changes take place. In fact, when the insects come out, they look exactly like their parents!

Before this life cycle can begin, a male and a female must mate. Then, the female lays her eggs. Flea eggs are small, white ovals. A female flea can lay up to 20 eggs per day on her host's hair. Shortly after they are laid, the eggs fall off the host. They usually land in the host's bed or other places the host rests.

Most fleas lay up to 500 eggs in their lifetime. Under perfect conditions, all their young would survive to reproduce. That means a single pair's extended family could grow to 20 trillion fleas in a year!

**BUG BYTES**

A newly hatched adult flea needs to eat right away. Otherwise, it will only survive for a few days.

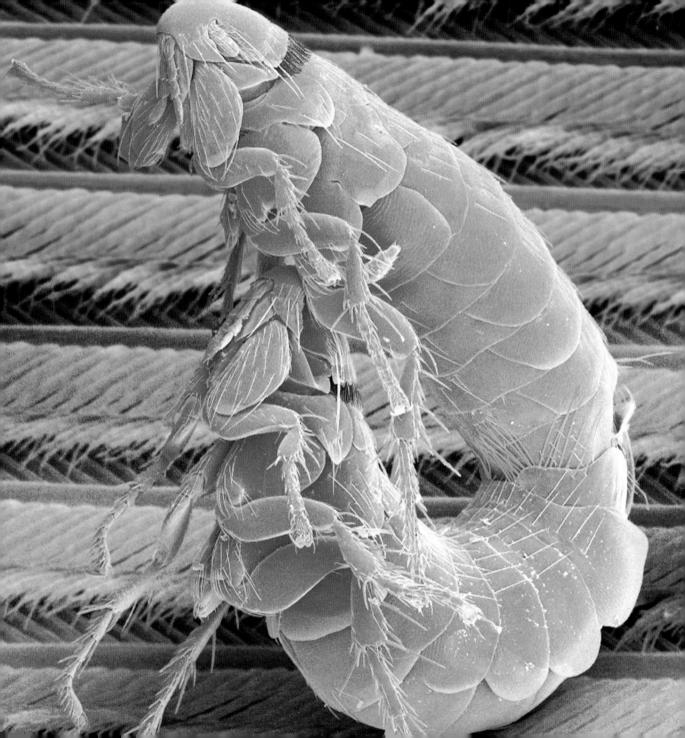

Once laid, flea eggs take 2 to 12 days to hatch. This length of time depends on the temperature and the moisture in the air. Warm weather encourages the eggs to hatch quickly. Cold weather has the opposite effect.

Hairy, wormy larvae emerge from the eggs. They immediately begin eating and growing. Soon, each larva grows out of its own skin. The exoskeleton splits and a new, larger larva comes out. This process is called molting. Flea larvae molt two to three times before they enter the next stage.

When the larvae complete their final molt, they weave cocoons around themselves. This is the pupal stage. During this stage, the larvae transform from wormy creatures into fully grown fleas. The pupae develop in their cocoons for 5 to 14 days. However, the transformed fleas do not emerge right away. Instead, they wait for a signal to come out.

What's the signal? An adult flea remains in its cocoon until it feels the vibrations of a possible host. The waiting period can last more than one year! When the adult does sense a host, it breaks out of its cocoon to hop on. The adult immediately starts to feed and reproduce. This begins the flea life cycle all over again.

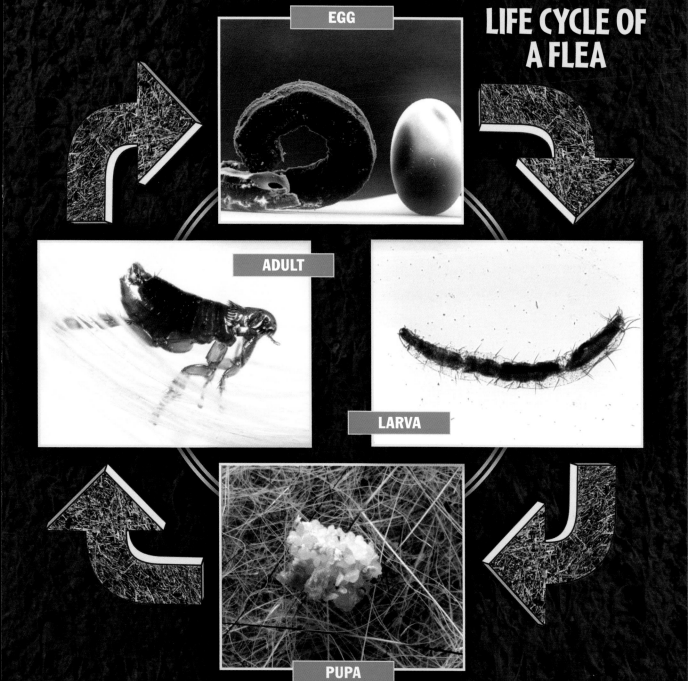

LIFE CYCLE OF A FLEA

EGG

ADULT

LARVA

PUPA

# Home Sweet Host

Fleas are **ectoparasites** that make their homes on many living creatures. They live in the hair, fur, or feathers of their host animal. Their names often describe the hosts they are found on. Such names include cat flea, bird flea, rat flea, and human flea. Can you guess where these fleas live?

Despite their names, many fleas like one host as well as the next. For example, dog fleas prefer members of the canine family. But, they will settle for Fluffy the cat. Rodent fleas make their homes on rats and mice. They will also live on some birds.

While between hosts, an adult flea will rest in many locations. Clothing, a couch, a dog bed, or a bird's nest are a few examples. These are also good places for a pupa to wait for a host.

Fleas find ways to survive in many types of **environments**. They can be found all around the world. However, they are more common in warm locations. No wonder so many of them like the inside of your house!

*Fleas love to bite where they can't be reached. This includes under a pet's collar or in its ears!*

# A Simple Diet

By now you know what fleas eat. They love to eat blood! In fact, an adult flea eats only blood. It likes to fill its gut with this juicy meal every day.

After eating a big meal, fleas often mate and lay eggs. Some species lay eggs on their host. Others jump off their host to lay their eggs. Either way, the eggs usually end up in the host's favorite resting spot. Soon, larvae come out. The blind, wormy creatures are very hungry! Luckily, they hatched right in larvae food.

What do larvae eat? They eat special waste products left behind by their parents. This is partly **digested** blood from the adult flea's meal. Flea larvae eat other snacks, too. Choices include hair, dead skin, feathers, and food particles.

Everything a flea eats passes through its three-part digestive system. The first part is called the foregut. This is where food enters the flea's body. From there, food travels to the midgut, or stomach. There, food is broken down and absorbed. Then, waste is released from the hindgut.

Flea waste is a necessary part of a larva's diet. Some of this waste will dry on the host's skin. Then it is called flea dirt.

# Fleas and You

Though fleas are tiny, they can be dangerous to your health. That is because some flea species carry and transmit disease. Plague is one dangerous disease transmitted by fleas.

Plague comes from rats. When rat fleas drink rat blood, they become carriers of this disease. Humans bitten by these fleas become **infected**. Hundreds of years ago, **bubonic plague** was known as the Black Death. It caused millions of deaths in Europe.

Typhus and tapeworms are other diseases carried by fleas. Rat fleas carry typhus. This disease causes high fever, body pain, and **rashes**. It can even lead to death.

Tapeworms are **parasites** commonly found in dogs. But, they can also affect humans. After a host swallows an infected flea, tapeworms grow in the host's intestine. Tapeworms are not as

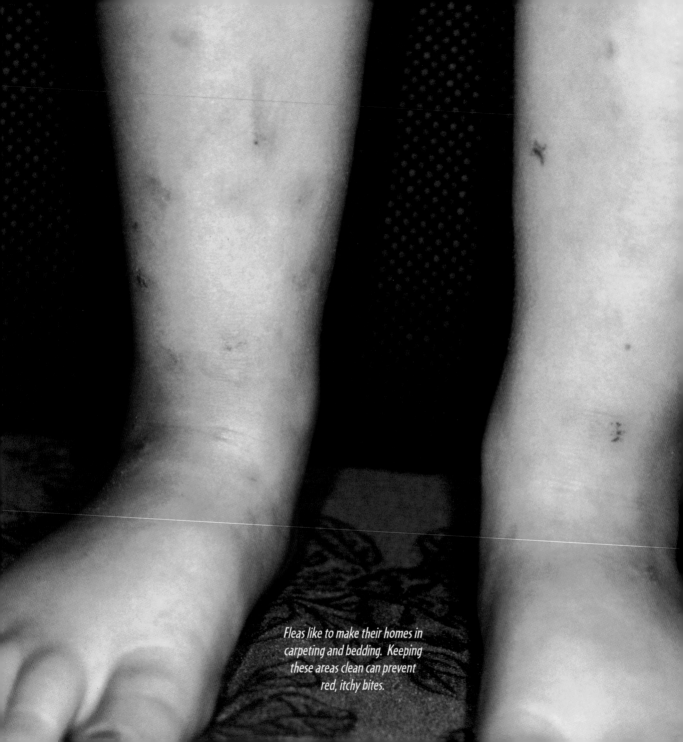

Fleas like to make their homes in carpeting and bedding. Keeping these areas clean can prevent red, itchy bites.

dangerous as some other diseases. However, they are still not something you want in your body.

Despite these dangers, most fleas are simply annoying. They can make your family's pet miserable. These crawling **ectoparasites** and their **saliva** can make a host's skin itch. The bites may or may not hurt. But, they will probably leave **welts**.

If the fleas hop onto you, you'll be miserable too! Some people may have an allergic reaction to a flea's bite. This results in **rashes** and hives. Sores can also result from excessive scratching. Open sores can become **infected**, causing more problems.

Luckily, fleas do have a few natural predators. These help control the flea population. Very small soil worms called nematodes are one flea predator. These worms love to eat flea larvae. And, they do not cause harm to people, animals, plants, or homes. Ants are another effective predator. These insects prey on flea eggs.

EAST GRAND FORKS CAMPBELL LIBRARY

An estimated $6 billion is spent each year on flea control in the United States.

# Fight the Bite

The misery caused by fleas is worth fighting. The best way to avoid them is simple. Reduce a flea's chances of surviving in your **environment**.

Keep your yard clean and trimmed. This will give fleas fewer places to hide. Admire wild animals from a distance. They probably have fleas! Think twice before cuddling with stray animals, too. All of these precautions will increase the distance between fleas and you.

Fleas are mostly outdoor insects. But they can **infest** homes, too. The best way to keep fleas away is to make your space

*Regular grooming is the first step to preventing fleas from infesting your pets. Bathe them and comb their fur with a flea comb.*

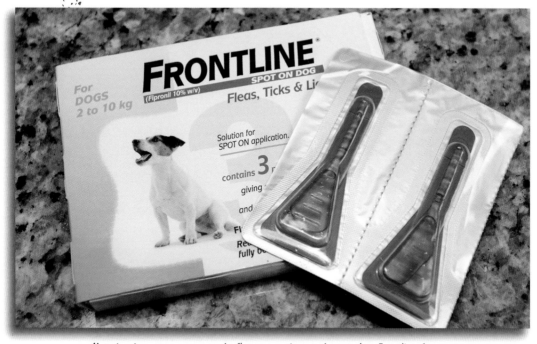

Veterinarians may recommend a flea-prevention product, such as Frontline, for your pet. This application kills flea larvae and pupae before they can mature into adult fleas.

less appealing! This means keeping your house clean, especially your pet's favorite places. Vacuumed floors, furniture, and bedding offer less food and fewer hiding spots for fleas.

You now know a lot about fleas. They are bloodsucking **ectoparasites**. They prefer to live on animals, but they will also jump onto you. Luckily, knowing how to discourage fleas will help keep those pesky bugs away!

# Glossary

**bubonic plague** - a disease that spreads by contact. It is marked by chills, fever, weakness, and swollen glands called buboes.

**complex** - having many parts, details, ideas, or functions.

**digest** - to break down food into substances small enough for the body to absorb. The process of digesting food is carried out by the digestive system.

**ectoparasite** - a parasite that lives outside its host's body. A parasite is an organism that lives off of another organism of a different species.

**environment** - all the surroundings that affect the growth and well-being of a living thing.

**infection** - the causing of an unhealthy condition by something harmful, such as bacteria or parasites. If something has an infection, it is infected.

**infest** - to spread or exist in large numbers so as to cause trouble or harm.

**inject** - to forcefully introduce a substance into something.

**metamorphosis** - the process of change in the form and habits of some animals during development from an immature stage to an adult stage.

**nerve** - one of the stringy bands of nervous tissue that carries signals from the brain to other organs.

**organ** - a part of an animal or a plant that is composed of several kinds of tissues and that performs a specific function. The heart, liver, gallbladder, and intestines are organs of an animal.

**rash** - a breaking out of the skin with red spots.

**saliva** - a liquid produced by the body that keeps the mouth moist.

**segment** - any of the parts into which a thing is divided or naturally separates.

**spine** - a stiff, pointed projection on an animal.

**welt** - a raised ridge or lump on the body.

# How Do You Say That?

**antennae** - an-TEH-nee
**bubonic plague** - byoo-BAH-nihk PLAYG
**epipharynx** - ehp-uh-FAR-ingks
**ganglia** - GANG-glee-uh
**hemolymph** - HEE-muh-lihmf
**laciniae** - luh-SIHN-ee-ee
**larvae** - LAHR-vee
**metamorphosis** - meh-tuh-MAWR-fuh-suhs
**nematodes** - NEH-muh-tohdz
**ocelli** - oh-SEH-leye
**pupae** - PYOO-pee
**Siphonaptera** - seye-fuh-NAHP-truh
**tracheae** - TRAY-kee-ee

# Web Sites

To learn more about fleas, visit ABDO Publishing Company on the World Wide Web at **www.abdopublishing.com**. Web sites about fleas are featured on our Book Links page. These links are routinely monitored and updated to provide the most current information available.

# Index